Managing for Daily Improvement in Healthcare

Author **Robert H. Goldsmith**

Contents

Foreword

I had the pleasure of working with Mr. Goldsmith to design and implement a patient-centered medical home. Mr. Goldsmith worked with our practice leadership team and staff to redefine roles and responsibilities for every level of staff, to reconfigure space and develop new flow systems for patients and information alike. While developing the content of these changes was complex and difficult, the greatest challenge during transformation was "managing through the change." Standard performance management strategies-- like setting clear expectations, providing transparent feedback and holding people accountable--while necessary were insufficient on their own to foster the engagement and critical thinking required in Lean process improvement and in transformation. Following many of the principles laid out in this book, our leadership team adopted "managing for daily improvement" to connect our daily work to higher level organizational goals, to promote problem solving among our staff, and to sustain our process changes. Using these strategies has been critical to our progress in building a patient-centered medical home thus far, and we see managing for daily improvement as our way forward to achieve even greater success in the future.

Mr. Goldsmith has the rare ability to teach complicated concepts in a plain-spoken and direct style that connects the learner to the critical elements of the lesson. To some, Lean language and culture may seem inaccessible. Mr. Goldsmith demystifies the Lean process of managing for daily improvement in this text, spelling out its key elements and outlining tactics for implementing this structured management system.

Over the course of my work with Mr. Goldsmith, he repeatedly emphasized that Lean leaders are most effective not when they provide solutions to problems, but rather when they ask questions that seek to expand the understanding and critical thinking of their people. In this book, Mr. Goldsmith remains true to form, continually challenging the reader with questions that demand reflection about current management process. By the end, Mr. Goldsmith has led the reader through a process of self-discovery about the value of managing for daily improvement. Perhaps of even greater benefit, those who diligently work through his work-book style questions will be able to take the first solids steps on the path to implementation.

Enjoy the journey!

Dr. Thad Schilling, MD

Chief of Internal Medicine at Harvard Vanguard Medical Associates Medford practice and

Medical Director of the Patient Centered Medical Home at Harvard Vanguard Medical Associates

Dedication

———

I would like to dedicate this book to my wife Cindy and my daughter Allison. Without their love and support throughout my career the contents of this book would have never been possible.

Being a Road Warrior isn't easy. Traveling every week and being away from home can take a toll on your family. My wife's and daughter's understanding has made it possible for me to do what I love to do and work with special organizations and their employees to make some extraordinary improvements within their processes.

They have supported me throughout my career and have been by my side through thick and thin. Cindy and Allie, thank you.

Acknowledgements

I would like to thank these particular individuals who helped with their input and knowledge in preparing this book.

Kurt Knoth, Vice President Performance Improvement, Spectrum Health.

Scott Brubaker, Chief Operation Officer, True Penny People North America

Steve Bullock, Plant Manager, Armstrong Wood Flooring

Introduction

———

Managing for Daily Improvement in Healthcare takes a direct approach on discussing the components of a Lean management system. My intent in this book is to bring a sensei's perspective and coach you on the particular methodologies and tools to help your organization be successful in sustaining gains.

Managing for Daily Improvement in Healthcare is a how-to book. I've seen other sensei's in my career that were afraid to give up their "secret sauce." With that said, I'm not stating this is the secret sauce. However, one sensei's humble opinion and experiences that have proven successful in sustaining gains while other organizations have failed.

This book lays out the components of the Managing for Daily Improvement (MDI) system, and it describes specific tools and how to use them in your own system to be effective.

If you are a leader in an organization that is embarking on or actively involved in Lean transformation, this book will help you understand the commitment and engagement level needed to take your organization to the next level.

To make a Lean transformation successful, an organization must be "all in". Half-hearted commitment from the Leadership group and middle management will not result in success. It is a hard and very noble journey, but it requires total agreement on the vision and the effort required to succeed.

Traditional Management Systems

To begin with, I would like to ask, "What type of management system do you have in place today?" Would you even call it a "system" or "process"? How do you accomplish the following tasks?

- Managing your daily operations
- Dealing with daily issues
- Working on daily improvements
- Sustaining previous improvements

Ask yourself: "are Leaders roles and responsibilities written, trained and followed"? If not, consistent outcomes for the organization may be problematic.

In my tenure as a Lean consultant and while working with many different clients, I've learned that most leaders don't have a daily management system in place to deal with these issues. If I had to characterize this behavior (or management style); I would call it "flying by the seat of your pants." Once again, this is an indication of the opportunities that managing for daily improvement is extremely important.

If I had to guess, I would bet that the majority of today's leaders don't have daily standard work that they follow. I'm not talking about detailed, step-by-step processes that you follow but rather a checklist of tasks that must be covered or observed on a daily basis.

Allow me to cover some of these tasks, and ask yourself if they sound familiar.

Prioritizing schedules. In the course of your day, do you have to ensure what people are doing or what parts, products, or services needs to be orchestrated in order to meet your customer's demands?

Chasing problems. Do you continually chase issues and problems? Do these issues and problems occur day after day?

Firefighting. Have you ever had to drop everything you were doing and "put out a fire" (not literally)? This is when something comes up and all operational motion stops until leadership addresses it or makes a decision to continue. Think how much time is "stolen" from you on a daily basis because you must join the "firefight" to solve the unexpected issue. Imagine your day having the discipline to reduce the firefights to an absolute minimum.

Searching for materials and equipment. Do you ever go looking for materials, supplies, or equipment? Have you ever been getting ready to perform some type of function and then realize that you don't have what you need?

Attending meetings. How many meetings do you attend on a daily basis? I'm sure they're all important! My favorite is having a meeting to plan for an upcoming meeting. I also love going to a meeting with no set agenda and no targeted output. Hello!

In your current management system, how much time, if any, is spent per day on identifying waste in your processes?

Most of these questions are rhetorical, but if you think through them, you'll understand how much valuable time is being wasted or not used properly.

Sensei Tip

Leaders must evaluate if they even have a management system in place and how effective that system is. Ensure that this system includes daily standard work. If it doesn't, develop and incorporate it immediately.

Sensei Question

Name the key elements that you currently have in your management system.

_____

_____

_____

_____

_____

_____

Do you currently have daily standard work, and if so, what are the key elements of that standard work?

_____

_____

_____

_____

_____

_____

Name the key elements (or issues) that pull you away from your standard work.

_____

_____

_____

_____

_____

_____

What Is Managing for Daily Improvement?

Managing for Daily Improvement (MDI) is a management system or approach for managing and sustaining continuous improvement initiatives. This becomes the key element to any organization's Lean strategy or continuous improvement process. It's part of a Lean infrastructure.

MDI is visual management for leaders to understand at a glance. This allows leaders to know if their organization is winning or losing in their strategy to transform their organization. MDI is a system for leaders to get close to where the work is being done (gemba), understand how the process improvements impact the area, and see if sustainment is occurring.

Key elements of MDI include the following:

- Visual management boards
- Daily huddles
- Daily audits
- Golden Tickets
- Leadership daily standard work

- Daily gemba walks
- Daily problem solving

MDI includes visual management of key performance indicators , daily team huddles, and solving daily issues immediately.

MDI huddles provide an opportunity to think about solving problems collaboratively. They occur daily and last five to ten minutes, and every level of staff is asked to attend and is encouraged to participate. The visual management boards that display the key performance indicators become a central place for communicating changes, successes, issues, and initiate "daily" problem solving. . The beauty of the MDI daily huddle is that it builds a sense of teamwork in the department.

Other components of MDI include gemba walks (going to where the work is and observing processes to identify waste), adherence to standard work (audits), daily-problem solving, and corrective action.

In my tenure as a Lean consultant, I have been asked too many times, "Why can't we sustain the improvements that we put in place?" I wholeheartedly believe that leaders can't sustain gains because they haven't implemented an MDI approach for daily continuous improvement.

A Lean management system consists of discipline, daily practices, and tools. You need to establish and maintain a persistent, intensive focus on processes. The focus sustains and extends Lean implementation. Little by little, almost unnoticeably, a Lean culture grows from the practices as they become habitual. A Lean culture emerges as leaders replace the mindset learned in batch-and-queue environments.[1]

A key reminder of the challenge is that most of current Leadership within an organization has been promoted due to their ability to "firefight". This "trait" is tough to forget; the Lean transformation's goal shall be to eliminate these unexpected and unwanted "owner of our time".

Sensei Tip

To sustain the gains and improve on a daily basis, your organization must incorporate a visual management system so that leaders understand at a glance if they are winning or losing the battle of transforming the organization. There is no status quo. You're either winning or you're losing. As a leader; you must become intolerant to losing.[2]

---

1 David W. Mann, *Creating a Lean Culture* (Boca Raton, FL: CRC Press, 2005), 5.

2 Bill Gaw, *Bill Gaw's Lean Manufacturing and Six Sigma Bulletin*, 2000–2013, http://bbasicsllc.com.

Sensei Questions

Name the key areas of your organization where you have visual management in place.

_____

_____

_____

_____

_____

_____

For these key areas, is it easy to understand at a glance if you are winning or losing?

_____

_____

_____

_____

_____

_____

How often do you visit these visual management areas, and what do you do with the information they provide?

_____

_____

_____

_____

_____

_____

What Is a Culture?

The key to cultural transformation is to understand what a culture is, how cultures emerge, and what drives cultures to change.

Culture is the sum of attitudes, customs, and behaviors that characterize the functioning of a group or organization. The members of a culture share certain ideas that shape their lives and behavior. Although there are thousands or maybe millions of different cultures, they all emerge in the same way and have shared core elements.

Emergence

Cultures emerge when shared thoughts become shared words. These become shared actions, and shared actions become shared habits, which become shared characteristics. This results in a defined culture.

Thoughts > Words > Actions > Habits > Characteristics > Culture

Once emerged, all cultures share these core elements:

- Language or other forms of communication
- Social and cultural expression
- Shared principles, beliefs, and thoughts

Cultural Change

Every culture changes over time, although the rate of change varies. The common key drivers of cultural change are as follows:

- Interaction (migration or invasion)
- New technologies
- Enlightenment (information and knowledge)
- Social thinking that undergoes transition

Evaluation

Regardless of where an organization wishes to start, the process is the same. It starts with seeking to understand.

Thoughts. What is your organization trying to accomplish? What is your business case for change?

Words. Are you communicating verbally or with writing, charts, visual aids, etc.? How do you know that these tools are working?

Actions. What is being done? What tools are being employed to accomplish your goals? How does the organization follow up to ensure compliance? What are the consequences for non-compliance?

Habits. Are tasks being done consistently? Is there continuity between processes? Are roles and responsibilities written, trained, sustained and audited?

Characteristics. What best describes your team/group? How is its morale? How would you describe your work environment?

Culture. Is your culture functional or dysfunctional?

Foundation Building

- What form or format of communication works best?
- What do the fundamental beliefs appear to be?
- What is working and what is not?
- What are the emotional hot spots?
- What within the culture is a critical part of the transformation?

Organizational Clarity. What are the key annual goals? How do they cascade down to my area?

Sensei Tip

For an organization to succeed in a Lean transformation, leaders must understand their culture and how they must impact that culture for change. When implementing an MDI approach, leaders must assess their organization's culture to understand its willingness to change. They can start communicating their expectations and vision through their personal behavior.

Sensei Questions

What key elements are needed in your communication plan, and what are the venues in which would you share this plan?

_____

_____

_____

_____

_____

_____

What are the organization's fundamental beliefs, and how can these beliefs influence a new vision and direction?

_____

_____

_____

_____

_____

What are your organization's current hot spots? What seems to be working or not working?

_____

_____

_____

_____

_____

_____

Why Promote MDI?

MDI unifies an organization's culture around a simple, systematic method for problem solving and continuous improvement. In any organization, it is paramount that the leadership adopts an approach for how to work through problems and determine resolutions to avoid recurrence. Organizations, divisions, and individuals frequently get so caught up in their day-to-day activities and "firefighting" that the problem-solving method is a quick fix that only temporarily solves the issue.

I understand the importance of a quick resolution to protect a patient, but more often than not, a quick fix is a Band-Aid (or workaround). A work-around normally doesn't address the direct or root cause, and the problem will likely rear its ugly head again.

The intent of MDI is to expose problems and make them transparent. What type of culture does your organization possess? Is it a culture that encourages individuals to make their problems transparent, or is it one that covers them up? (The problems may indicate that you are not doing a good job or, even worse, causing the problem.) The latter surely doesn't promote transparency.

The Toyota culture celebrates the identification of problems as "golden nuggets." Once a problem is recognized, the root cause can be determined and thus eliminated permanently. If you are not aware of a problem, how can you fix it?

From my twenty-five years of experience, I learned that all organizations have problems to deal with. Some organizations choose not to recognize them or don't promote a culture that makes them obvious. If you're looking to take your organization to the next level of performance, you must drive your culture to make every problem transparent. These "problems" being made transparent must be accepted as a "good thing".

If you believe that you are part of an organization that promotes transparency, can a stranger walk through your organization's gemba and know the following?

- What the top three problems are
- Which champion is working on the problems
- What action is taking place to resolve the problems

Sensei Tip

Too many organizations underestimate the power of visual management and/or making problems transparent. The first step in MDI is to incorporate an information area that makes your problems and an approach to address those problems transparent. There's no time like the present to start developing your information area. This book will help you design and implement your MDI approach.

Sensei Questions

Name the top three problems in your area.

_____

_____

_____

_____

_____

_____

Are they transparent, and if so, is a champion named? What corrective action is taking place?

_____

_____

_____

_____

_____

_____

How to Achieve MDI

———

True MDI is achieved when the area, unit, or department cannot do without it.

When you incorporate the metric boards (visual management boards with key performance indicators) and huddles, you will have to make it mandatory to attend the huddles. If this is not done, not many will attend. In other words, the people are "voluntold" to participate. After the area has been meeting daily for approximately three weeks, discussing daily operational problems and solving their issues, they will not want the huddle to go away. This is because they will see the benefit on how it makes their day better.

On the other hand, if the area members are willing to give up the daily routine to solve problems, there's probably a good chance that they are not using MDI properly. Leadership intervention will certainly be required.

I was with a client, conducting training for process improvement specialist, and I was going over the role of implementing MDI and coaching leadership on utilization. One specialist asked, "How long must we continue MDI?" The answer was, "Forever!"

I'm going to borrow an analogy from a colleague of mine, Ron Bercaw, the president of Breakthrough Horizons. As he explained it, MDI is like the instrument panel of your car. Are you ever ready to get rid of your instrument panel? How will you know how fast you are going? How will you know if you need gas? You get my point.

One of the key components of MDI is the power of observation or going to the gemba. I have seen many times where leadership doesn't visit the gemba enough. They make far too many decisions from their office or during a meeting without knowing what the real problem is. Sound familiar? Are you ever "guilty" of this?

So this is why the information centers or MDI boards are put in the area where the work is being done. It gets everyone close to the area where things are happening.

The next step is to incorporate a daily team huddle. Select a time that is conducive for as many attendees as possible. Leaders should make this huddle mandatory to ensure a high level of attendance at the beginning. It will also send a message that the leaders believe in this approach and that it is important.

Sensei Tip

Proper use of MDI helps your organization navigate day-to-day operations. As mentioned earlier, it's like your instrument panel of your car. Without it, how do you navigate your car? MDI should be the mechanism to navigate your day-to-day operations and solve the problems that reoccur.

Sensei Questions

Do you have a process that allows your staff to meet and discuss what the day looks like?

_____

_____

_____

_____

_____

_____

Are the people who attend this daily meeting excited to attend? If not, why not?

_____

_____

_____

_____

_____

_____

Board Transparency

One of the first steps to implementing MDI is to incorporate a metric tracking board where people huddle, discuss daily operational issues, and progress to daily problem solving.

Surprisingly, few organizations have their measures that truly "drive the proper behavior". Often the measures that are being utilized are either irrelevant to the specific area or a measure that the specific area has no opportunity of influencing. So before you begin setting up the MDI board, understand the importance of getting the measures **_correct_**.

The MDI board should follow a "balanced scorecard approach," which is used by Lean organizations to monitor long-term success. It uses a balance of business performance and human development measures. It is also referred to as "true north metrics." Another key point: the metrics needs to be easily obtainable. If they require manual collection on an hourly basis and hours to compute and compare, the metrics will eventually not be effective. Use finite measures whenever possible. If the measurement is "fluffy", the outcome will be "fluffy" as well.

These are the basic balanced scorecard approach categories.

Human Development (HD). Leaders empower staff at every level to make improvements in an environment that promotes excellence.

Safety (S). The organization provides care that is patient centered and safe, ensuring a safe workplace for staff.

Quality (Q). The organization provides care that is patient centered and effective; it ensures improved population health and high patient satisfaction.

Delivery (D). The organization meets or exceeds patients' expectations and needs for timely, value-added services.

Productivity (P). The organization uses all resources effectively and efficiently by removing work that does not add value.

Growth (G). The organization brings in new patients and offers more services to current patients.

I prefer that the MDI board to be set up so that each category has its own column. See figure 1 for an example of the board layout.

As you can see, each balanced scorecard metric category has its own column. Note that each column has an area to conduct a Pareto Analysis (see chapter 8) to understand why a metric may be trending in the wrong direction. The most critical area of the board is the problem-solving section and learning why your metric is trending in the wrong direction.

MDI Board				
People	Safety	Quality	Delivery	Cost
problem statement	potential causes	Corrective Action	Who___	When___

I particularly like the sample shown above because it limits the number of problems an area is working on at one time. However, I have seen times when an organization used a "Kaizen Newspaper" in each separate column to solve a problem in each individual metric category (see figure 2).

Kaizen Newspaper

Area:

Date	Issue	Corrective Action	Status	Action By:	Target Date
			⊞		
			⊞		
			⊞		
			⊞		
			⊞		
			⊞		
			⊞		
			⊞		

Sensei Tip

When visiting the information center or the MDI board, observe the metrics, and determine if any of them are trending in the wrong direction. If so, has a Pareto Analysis been performed? More importantly, has the problem been defined and a corrective action assigned? If no written documentation appears on the board in the problem-solving section, a solution probably isn't being implemented. The problem-solving section or "Kaizen Newspaper" must be filled out, and a person must be assigned as the champion of that action.

Sensei Questions

Is there an area in your unit, department, or organization (preferably a high-traffic area) where you could hang a metric tracking board, or are the walls considered sacred ground? If the staff would rather not see a board hung there, why?

_____

_____

_____

_____

_____

_____

Is your organization ready to be so transparent with its problems that you allow your patients to view the issues? Please explain your organization's readiness.

_____

_____

_____

_____

_____

_____

Metric Selecting and Tracking

As mentioned in the last chapter, you should use the balanced scorecard approach and be tracking metrics in each category. Since this is managing for daily improvement, think of metrics that are important to you on a daily basis, not weekly or monthly.

Metric selecting

When selecting a metric, it's important to understand the difference between a *driver metric* and a *watch metric*. A driver metric usually compels some type of activity to take place. A watch metric follows the trend from the action of the driver metric.

Driver metrics. This data is collected daily or hourly, which helps you manage *to* results, not *by* results. Generally, the driver metric is changing your behavior to do something to affect the watch metric.

Let me give you an example. When I turned forty, things started to fall apart. My eyesight was impaired, my blood pressure was rising, and my cholesterol was high. Reading glasses took care of the first problem, and Lisinopril took care of my high blood pressure.

However, I could change my behavior (driver metric) to affect my high cholesterol (watch metric).

The watch metric was the lipid panel results of my total cholesterol, which was at 250. My driver metric was my behavior change that I would have to make to get my total cholesterol score under 200. My behavior change was to exercise thirty minutes a day and cut down on saturated fat at each meal.

So I tracked my daily thirty-minute workouts and my saturated fat intake. I had two reasons to track the metric: to ensure that I was doing the behavioral change and to ensure that my metric was trending in the right direction *from* my behavior change. I'm proud to announce that my last cholesterol reading was 177, which is not too shabby.

Watch metrics. These are lag (wait or delay) indicators. Usually the watch metric is the result or effect of the driver metric. In the example above, the watch metric was getting my blood work done and the results from the lipid panel.

When deciding on what metric to track on your MDI board, ask what's important to you on a daily basis. What tells you whether you are having a good day or a bad day? Are you winning or losing today?

An important daily measure in a hospital's emergency department (ED) is its "elopement rate." How many patients leave the ED without being seen? The elopement rate, or Left Without Being Seen (LWBS) rate, is the watch metric or lag metric. In order for the ED staff to lower the elopement or LWBS rate, they have to drive some type of new behavior. For instance, they will have to lower the patient's wait time. The longer it takes for a patient to see a physician, the more likely it is that the patient will get impatient and leave without being seen.

A solution that one of my clients came up with in the MDI huddle was to move the triage nurse from "the back" in the exam rooms to "in front of" the registration area. As soon as the patient walked through the door of the ED, the triage nurse was right there to greet the patient and assess the severity of the situation.

Metric Tracking

When tracking your metrics, it's important to present them so that it's easy to understand. This includes understanding what you're tracking, what the goal of the metric is and how you are performing to reach it.

I'm a huge fan of daily, linear graphs with the goal specified with a green line, the intention being that all metrics trend up. If all the graphs trend in the same direction, it's easy to detect, even from far away, that a metric is *not* trending in the right direction, and this should pull you to the board to investigate (see figure 3).

Which metric or category should you focus on?

I recommend using a red-and-green magnetic dot beside the metric graph to help you visualize or give another indication of good or bad trends (see figure 4).

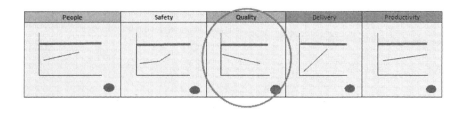

Did you pick the "Quality" metric above? As you can see in the example, all the metrics should trend up. The goal is indicated by a green line, and I have created andons with red and green dots. Not only do you have the trend line going down, but the red dot indicates that there is a problem with this metric. A Pareto Analysis must be done to understand why.

I often run into people who like to make Excel spreadsheets and graphs and post them on the board. I'm not a big fan of this method. Many times after the spreadsheet is created, populated, and posted on the board, that's all it is—a posting!

I believe there's power in making the owner of the metric go to the graph on the board, manually post the performance of the day, and connect the trend line between points. It gets people to the Gemba, and they'll feel the pain and see immediately if the trend is going in the wrong direction.

You might ask, "Aren't all of these visuals a lot to maintain?" They are not time consuming if there is a systematic process for maintaining them. In fact, that is one of the main contributions of standard work for leaders. Team leaders do or do not make entries on the visual trackers as specified by their individual standardized work. The standard work of supervisors and value stream leaders directs them to review the visual controls several times a day (at least once a day, for value stream leaders) for two reasons: to verify that the visuals are being maintained and to verify that appropriate actions have been initiated when abnormal conditions are identified [3]

Visuals amount to wallpaper if they are not taken seriously and used for action. Without disciplined follow-up by leaders, visuals are destined to take their dust-covered places behind equipment and under staircases along with the other boards and banners of failed initiatives. It is not a pretty picture, but it is a common one in healthcare organizations where leaders did not have the discipline to stay with the initiatives they launched.[4]

Sensei Tip

I highly recommend using a manual, linear graph and making the metric owners responsible for updating the metrics daily. Have all the metrics trend in the upward direction (hence, true north metrics). Red and green andon indicators will help transparency. The easier you make it, the more likely it is that it will be understood. If the board is understood, you have a better chance of it being used.

---

3 David W. Mann, *Creating a Lean Culture* (Boca Raton, FL: CRC Press, 2005), 61.

4 David W. Mann, *Creating a Lean Culture* (Boca Raton, FL: CRC Press, 2005), 46.

Sensei Questions

Can you name a watch metric in each category of the balanced scorecard approach that indicates whether you had a good day or a bad day?

_____

_____

_____

_____

_____

_____

Now can you name a driver metric that will affect each of those watch metrics to understand if you are having a good day or bad day?

_____

_____

_____

_____

_____

_____

Now that you have determined what metrics are important to know how you are performing, are these metrics easy to understand and easy to get? If not, what might be a better selection?

_____

_____

_____

_____

_____

_____

Pareto Analysis

———

After you have your metrics on the MDI board and are tracking them on a linear graph, it's critical to understand whether they are trending in the right direction. If they are not, you need to understand the leading indicators. This is where you begin your data analysis and construct a Pareto Analysis.

In the early 1900s, an Italian economist named Vilfredo Pareto created a mathematical formula to describe the unequal distribution of wealth in his country. His analysis showed that 20 percent of the people owned 80 percent of the land— hence the "80/20 Rule." Pareto Analysis, as it is known today, can be an effective tool to help you manage your organization.

I describe Pareto Analysis as a graphical form of collected data (see figure 5). It's compiling data and putting it in a visual form to quickly understand where the data is guiding you. Apply it when you need to understand where to focus your efforts and solve problems that keep occurring. You can also use it to help "clarify your problem.

Causes For Medications Not Being Delivered On-Time

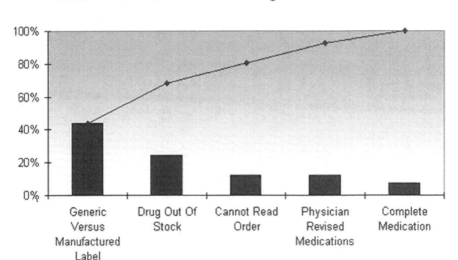

Pareto Analysis is a means of focusing effort on the areas that matter the most. It's a bar chart that shows the different causes of the problem. It's a robust means of drilling into data as far as you can go before using qualitative techniques. Use Pareto Analysis to avoid working on the wrong problem. Too many times people jump to conclusions about what they perceive a problem to be without analyzing the data. They tend to go by a gut feeling and believe that they know why they are experiencing the issue.

If you cannot explain your problem with data, it is more an opinion than an actual problem.

When conducting a problem-solving initiative, use a Pareto Analysis as soon as possible to narrow the focus. I highly recommend performing a data analysis to confirm that you and your team are on the right track.

To clarify the problem, start at the top level, and identify the vital categories (figure 6, circled area) that are approximately 20 percent of the total categories. These may add up to 80 percent of the total occurrences (hence the 80/20 Rule). Think of the "vital few" versus the "trivial many." I bet you can relate to 20 percent of your problems causing 80 percent of your issues or consuming 80 percent of your time.

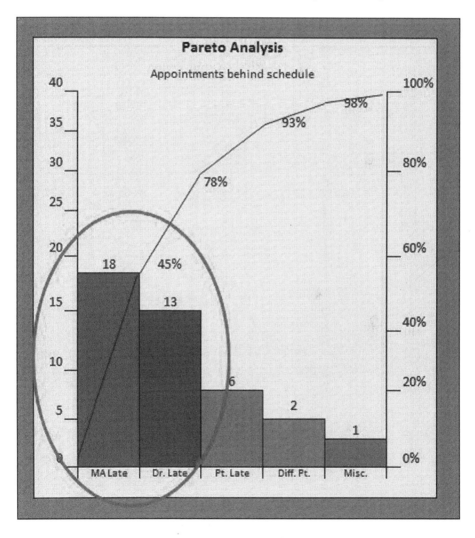

If your initial Pareto Analysis plot is flat, you may wish to try with another y-axis. For instance, if the original plot is focused purely on the number of units (as the example above indicates), think about changing the y-axis to incorporate time spent on or cost associated with each unit. You'll be surprised at how your plot may change by changing the y-axis.

It's not uncommon to go to three levels of Pareto Analysis before understanding which area to investigate. Many times I've seen organizations collect data at too high a level. I've run across categories such as "missing," "broken," or "loose" and even a broad category called "miscellaneous" (see figure 7).

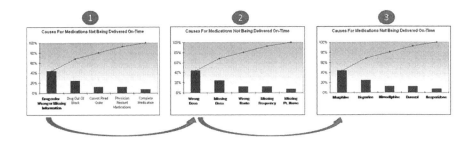

Per the example in figure 7, ask what is missing or what is wrong with the drug order. A deeper dive into the data is needed to understand what major contributor is making the drug order inaccurate.

All the drug orders with missing or wrong information were collected, and the second level of the Pareto Analysis was performed. The biggest bar (I refer to it as "the longest pole in the tent") shows that the dose was wrong on the majority of the orders.

A third level of Pareto Analysis is still needed to understand what medications seem to have a problem of getting the correct dosage. Per the example, morphine is the major contributor. The dosage has been incorrectly prescribed on the drug order, which results in the pharmacist doing due diligence to get it properly prescribed and taking too much time to fill the medication order and administer it to the patient. We have narrowed the focus to understand why the morphine orders continue to have wrong or missing doses.

Sensei Tip

Pareto Analysis is simple and one of the most effective tools to break down a problem. I highly recommend using this tool as soon as possible when clarifying your problem or business case. It will ensure that you and your team are on the right track.

Sensei Questions

How much data analysis do you do as part of your current problem-solving process?

_____

_____

_____

_____

_____

_____

How does Pareto Analysis allow you to narrow your problem?

_____

_____

_____

_____

_____

_____

Huddles

MDI huddles provide an opportunity to think about solving problems collaboratively. Huddles occur daily and last five to ten minutes. Every level of staff is asked to attend and is encouraged to participate. The boards become a central place for communicating changes, successes, issues, and solutions.

I use the phrase "encouraged to participate" loosely. At the beginning, it isn't an option. Communicate to your staff that attending the huddle is mandatory. If you make it an option, you'll have poor attendance. The staff members don't know what it is and will be reluctant to take the time out of their daily routine. I recommend that your attendance list include the physicians.

You'll need to pick a time during the day that will ensure higher attendance and doesn't disrupt the work that needs to be done. This must be a standard time. If it changes daily, it's like a moving target. Your team won't know when to attend, and again, you'll end up with low attendance.

The huddle is intended to be short. If you have to, set a timer, and when it goes off, the huddle is over. If you allow the huddle to last fifteen to thirty minutes, it becomes painful and will affect productivity.

If you run more than one shift, have at least one huddle per shift. If you run three shifts, have at least three huddles. It's not uncommon to hold a couple of huddles per shift. Conduct one in the first half of the day and another in the second half of the day.

When you implement the huddle, it will be more of an information-sharing session, and that's okay. It will naturally progress into a daily problem-solving huddle.

Three Tiers of Daily Huddles

The daily accountability process takes place as an interlocking set of three brief, structured, daily huddles, one of which is the familiar but often misunderstood "team start-up huddle." Each huddle is an explicit example of a Lean operation's focus on comparing expected with actual.

There are three tiers of huddles:

1. The first tier (because it typically happens at the start of the shift) is the operation team leader's huddle with the team members.

2. The second is the supervisor huddle with his or her team leaders and any dedicated support group representatives.

3. The third-tier huddle is with the value stream manager (or equivalent) and his or her supervisors and support group representative or staff members.[5]

---

5 David W. Mann, *Creating a Lean Culture* (Boca Raton, FL: CRC Press, 2005), 46.

The tier huddle approach is intended for "next-level-up interaction." It gives the team leader an opportunity to interact with the team, the supervisor an opportunity to interact with the team lead, and the manager an opportunity to interact with the supervisor. It is the perfect opportunity to escalate problems to the next level if needed.

Sensei Tip

Do not allow the huddle to become a complaint session. It is too easy to allow that to happen, and it will be counterproductive. You'll start to see members avoiding the huddle and not participate, and then nobody wins. The subject matter must be the important issues that might affect their day, or they will lose interest quickly. If you are going to lead the huddle, prepare yourself with notes, and bring the team in for collaboration to resolve those issues and make it a good day.

Sensei Questions

When is a good time for each shift to hold their huddles? What time would ensure a high attendance?

_____

_____

_____

_____

_____

_____

Name a couple of topics that your team would want to discuss on a day-to-day basis to understand how operations are performing and why.

_____

_____

_____

_____

_____

_____

Getting Started

The beautiful thing about being in a Lean culture is that you don't have to wait for perfection to try something out. This applies to implementing MDI as well.

In an earlier chapter, I talked about using the balanced scorecard approach. Allow me talk about metric selection at early implementation. It's okay to start with a narrow focus and limit the number of metrics you are tracking. You don't want to overwhelm your team, so start on a small scale.

For example, maybe your safety record isn't meeting your target, and that's your primary focus. So start with the safety column, whether it is OSHA recordables, an incident rate, or ISIS reporting. Create a linear graph with a target for where you want to be, and start tracking.

Maybe you're experiencing a lot of errors or defects with the service that your team provides. Start with the quality column, and track the metric that's critical to your customer (the patients). At the beginning, it's okay to start small or have a narrower focus.

Whatever column you choose to start with, remember to graph the metric, use Pareto Analysis to understand where the majority of the problems are coming from, and begin your daily operation discussions at the huddle.

Leading the Huddle

At first, your supervisor or team leader should lead the huddle. After the team becomes comfortable with the MDI process, the leader can pass the baton. At the beginning, have a backup for your supervisor so that if he or she is not available, someone else will take over. Eventually you want to get as many people as possible on your team to lead the huddle. As they become familiar with the process, you'll want them to own it.

The leader must be prepared for the huddle. At the end or beginning of the shift, the MDI board must be updated for potential issues and the huddle discussion topics decided. Again, make sure that the huddle leader is well prepared for what will be covered with the team prior to the huddle. Do not try to cover every aspect presented on the board, especially after you've implemented the balanced scorecard approach. There isn't enough time to cover everything. Remember that the huddle is intended to last five to ten minutes, so you may want to assign different topics for different days. For example, Mondays are for safety and kamishibai, Tuesdays are for quality and Golden Tickets, Wednesdays are for...I'm sure you get the idea.

If you're wondering what kamishibai and Golden Tickets are, I have purposely not discussed those processes yet. As mentioned earlier, start out with a narrow focus, and don't wait for perfection. At the beginning, I don't recommend having "everything" in place.

(I explain kamishibai and the Golden Tickets in later chapters.) A wise man once said, "Perfection kills many good ideas. A 50 percent solution today is better than an 85 percent solution six months from now."

As trivial as this may sound, go from left to right, and highlight the areas on the board that you want to discuss. I was with my client, and the supervisor kept jumping around on the board, making it difficult for the team to stay focused. It also made it difficult for the supervisor to keep track of what he had discussed and where he was going next. Go from left to right, and be prepared prior to the huddle.

Sensei Tip

To captivate your huddle audience, you need to discuss topics of personal interest. Otherwise the team members will become uninterested and stop coming to the huddle. Determine what topics your team will need to know in order to have a good day. Pull them into the conversation for better engagement. I highly encourage you to include the physicians!

Sensei Questions

Can you name a couple key metrics that you are already tracking that might be good choices for narrowing your focus? If so, explain why.

_____

_____

_____

_____

_____

_____

Can you describe some key operational topics that your team might want to discuss on a daily basis to ensure that issues are being covered? If so, explain why.

_____

_____

_____

_____

_____

_____

Kamishibai
(Kah-mee-she-bye)

Several years ago, I was conducting a gemba walk with a site administrator, the operation manager, and the internal medicine supervisor. While reviewing the MDI board, I saw that a key metric on "physician in-basket management" was trending in the wrong direction.

Once you realize that a process isn't performing to expectations, the first question to ask is, "Does standard work exist?" If the answer is yes, ask, "Are you following standard work?" If the answer is no, proceed with the third question, "Why aren't we following the standard work?" The final question to ask is, "Is the standard work correct?"

I asked my client's leadership these questions. It was determined that standard work did exist. However, the alarming answer to the next question was that they were unsure if the standard work was being followed. So I continued with the investigation and asked, "How often do you audit the processes to know if they are following the standard work or not?" The even more alarming answer was that they didn't conduct any audits!

If audits weren't conducted on the standard work, the people probably would not follow the new standard work. It was evident that a simple audit system was needed immediately.

As part of the Toyota production system, kamishibai is used as a visual control for performing audits within a process. A series of cards (see figure 8) is placed on a board or in a box and selected at random by the area leadership. This ensures that processes are being followed to standard work, the workplace is maintained, and quality checks are being performed.[6]

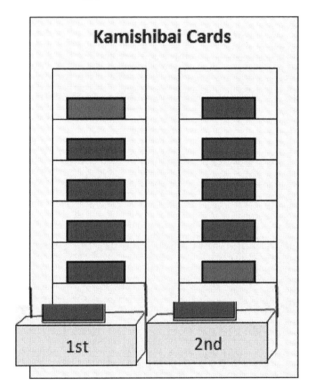

6 "Lean Manufacturing Blog, Kaizen Articles and Advice," Gemba Panta Rei, retrieved 10/7/2013.

The standardized approach of the kamishibai routine audits minimizes differences between the individual preference, style, or attention to detail. This reduces variability in the outcome of the audit.

The kamishibai board placement also helps focus the leader's attention inside the gemba. To be an effective leader and ensure that standard work is being followed, you need to go to the gemba, take a card (see figure 9), and follow the instructions. It's humbling when you think about it. The kamishibai process standardizes and prescribes the audits for standard work.

Card #3
OP Pharmacy

Expired/Short dated Medications

When to audit: Anytime
Approximate length of audit: 5 minutes

Expectation: Area is to be kept Straightened throughout each day. If employee is currently working in the space it should still be apparent if criteria below are sustaining.

Please check for all of following:
- **Expired Meds Bin (Sample 5)**

Pass Criteria:
6S principles apply to the office.

1. Are there meds in the short dated bin which will not expire in the next 3 months?
2. Are the expired and short dated medications in their designated locations?
3. Have expired/short dated meds been returned on a monthly basis? (look at last 2 months)

6S PRINCIPLES
Process improvement

SORT – Remove non-essentials
STRAIGHTEN – Organize remaining items
SHINE – Clean, paint and polish work area
STANDARDIZE – Label and color code
SUSTAIN – Maintain changes, keep in order
SAFETY – Make it safe

Note: Check the items listed on this card to assess compliance. If good, insert the card into the slot with "green" side showing. If issues are found, please place card in slot with "red" showing and document corrective actions on board.

Card #3
OP Pharmacy

Expired/Short dated Medications

When to audit: Anytime
Approximate length of audit: 5 minutes

Expectation: Area is to be kept Straightened throughout each day. If employee is currently working in the space it should still be apparent if criteria below are sustaining

Please check for all of following:
- **Expired Meds Bin (Sample 5)**

Fail Criteria:
One or more of the following steps has been missed.

1. Meds in the short dated bin will not expire in the next 3 months
2. Expired and short dated medications are located in areas outside designated area
3. Expired/short dated meds were not returned monthly. (look at last 2 months)

Corrective Action: Let the staff know why they failed and provide details of failure on corrective action sheet on Kamishibai Board.

6S PRINCIPLES
Process improvement

SORT – Remove non-essentials
STRAIGHTEN – Organize remaining items
SHINE – Clean, paint and polish work area
STANDARDIZE – Label and color code
SUSTAIN – Maintain changes, keep in order
SAFETY – Make it safe

Note: Check the items listed on this card to assess compliance. If good, insert the card into the slot with "green" side showing. If issues are found, please place card in slot with "red" showing and document corrective actions on board.

An item that *must* be on the leader's daily standard work is to conduct at least two kamishibai audits: one in the morning and one in the afternoon, and it wouldn't hurt to do more.

The more audits that are performed daily, the more likely it is that the standard work will be followed. When leaders continue to be inside the gemba and observe whether processes are being followed, this demonstrates to the team that it is important to follow the standard work.

As mentioned earlier, the kamishibai process should be located in the gemba. I advise you to create a kamishibai board (see figure 10) next to your MDI metric board.

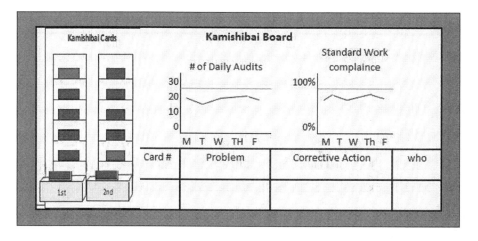

As you can see from the illustration, if the audit passes, the card is inserted with the green side showing. If the audit has failed (meaning that the team member did not follow the standard work described on the card), the card is inserted with the red side showing.

If the team member failed the audit, you need to capture the card number that failed on the corrective action section of the kamishibai board. Identify why the audit failed (problem), and most importantly, what are you doing (corrective action) to correct this situation so that your team member does not fail the audit again.

Each day, track how many audits are conducted and how many have passed. Track and trend both of these items on the kamishibai board as illustrated.

Sensei Tip

When an audit has failed, there's no time like the present to coach and mentor the individual who wasn't following the standard work. If you notice a trend on a piece of standard work where several individuals continually do not follow the process, ask yourself, "Is the standard work correct?" Get everyone involved in conducting the audits from the colleagues who perform the standard work all the way up to the area vice president.

Sensei Questions

Do you have an audit system in place? If not, how are you performing in output, safety, and quality?

_____

_____

_____

_____

_____

_____

If you have incorporated an audit system, how many audits are conducted per day? What is the compliance level, and what levels of leadership are conducting the audits?

_____

_____

_____

_____

_____

_____

Golden Tickets

About two years ago, I started supporting a catheterization lab value stream for a new client. One of our first initiatives was to improve the ability of on-time starts (first heart procedure of the day) and to lower the rate of table resets (setting the table for a particular heart procedure).

I recommended starting with a narrow focus versus targeting perfection and implementing all the elements that make up MDI. That's what we did. We focused on those top two metrics.

This value stream improved on-time starts from 25 percent to 75 percent and decreased weekly table resets from seven to zero, which was impressive. However, it became apparent early on that we needed to incorporate another element of MDI, because we were losing our audience.

The value stream team agreed that these were important initiatives to improve their performance, but after several weeks of discussing these topics during their daily huddles, it became monotonous. The team wanted to work on other issues that affected their daily work lives, so it was time to add the "Golden Ticket process" to their MDI.

The Golden Ticket process is similar to an employee suggestion program, but it focuses on problems that affect the area operations on a daily basis. It's called the Golden Ticket process because you have the team fill out a golden card (see figure 11) for each problem that continues to occur. We chose a golden card to follow Toyota's philosophy that problems are "golden nuggets."

Golden Ticket Improvement Opportunity			
Name:		Shift:	Date:
What is the problem?:			
Why is it happening?:			
Potential Solutions:			
Impact: (circle one) People, Safety, Quality, Delivery,			
Patient Satisfaction, or Cost			
Owner:			
Who:	What:		By when:
Complete date:			

We encourage everyone to fill out a golden ticket when they experience a recurring problem. Once the ticket is filled out, it is placed in the parking lot (dedicated place on the MDI board where the Golden Tickets wait) to be worked on. The next step is for the team to determine the impact of resolving the issue and how hard it will be to resolve. To determine these measures, I recommend using a PICK chart (see figure 12).

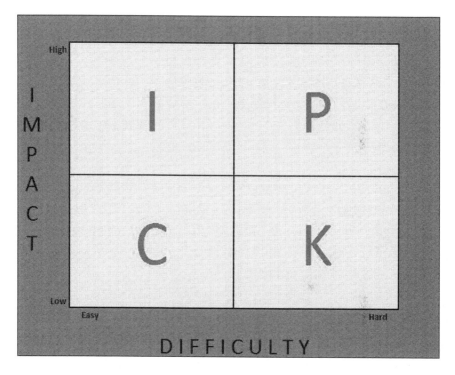

The four quadrants of the chart are labeled P, I, C, and K.

P stands for Plan to do. These activities are categorized as high impact but hard to do and will probably take longer, so they are "put on the back burner."

I stands for Implement. These activities are categorized as high impact and easy to do. When the solutions fall within this quadrant, they are usually the ones you choose to implement as soon as you can and move into the working lot (area on the MDI board identified as what the team will be working on).

C stands for Choose to do. These activities are categorized as low impact and easy to do. Your team will determine if it is worth the time and effort to work on the problem.

K stands for Kick out. These activities are categorized as low impact and hard to do. Anything within this quadrant is dropped or kicked off the chart because of the effort required to fix it (with a low impact).

The way to use the PICK chart is to have all the solution approaches written on a Golden Ticket, one solution per ticket. The huddle leader reads the Golden Ticket opportunity in front of the chart. The team members rate the solution's level of difficulty (or associated cost) as easy, medium, or hard.

The leader asks the members, "If we solve this problem, how big of an impact will it have on daily operations?" They rate the impact as low, medium, or high (see figure 13). It's a simple yet effective tool.

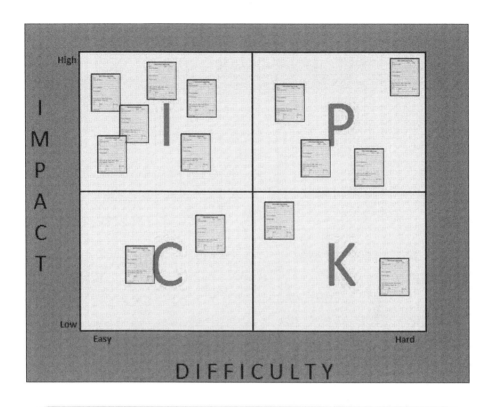

Sensei Tip

The intent of the Golden Ticket process is that they are small in scope so that the team members can work on implementing solutions in a timely fashion. The team members should turn in ideas to improve their work area, and the best case scenario is when a process is implemented by the person who had the idea.

Sensei Questions

How are suggestions from your team members handled?

_____

_____

_____

_____

_____

_____

Do you have a formal way to track suggestions implemented, and do your team members feel that their voices are being heard?

_____

_____

_____

_____

_____

_____

Process Control Boards

One of the most effective visual management tools is the process control board (PCB), but when starting your Lean journey, it seems like pulling teeth to get them implemented.

Earlier in my career when I was value stream manager for a medical device company, I was walking the gemba of our remanufactured hospital bed assembly process. I stopped at the PCB and was reviewing the performance data when the team lead approached me and said, "Bob, you are the only person around here who pays attention to that board." I knew that we had problem!

My supervisor was walking down the aisle, and I called him over. I asked if he had reviewed the board lately, and the answer was no. I also asked him if he realized that they missed several bed shipments last week, all for the same reason (Pareto Analysis).

This was a coaching moment for me and my supervisor on the importance of the PCB. It is one of the most effective visual management tools if used properly! When my supervisor understood why we had missed the shipments, we knew we needed to develop a corrective action.

The PCB is intended to go directly into the cell where you are producing the product or service that you provide. It's also known as an "hour-by-hour chart," because you analyze your performance every hour.

Too many times I get the push back that hour-by-hour analysis is overkill and that teams can run a report at the end of the day to tell them how they did. This is missing the point. If they know early that they have a problem and what is causing the problem, there is a good chance that they can fix it and turn the day around.

The board should state what the plan of output is, what is produced or provided, whether there is a variance between the two, and, if so, what caused the variance (see figure 14).

Sensei Tip

As mentioned, at first, it will feel like pulling teeth to get the boards implemented, but as a leader, you must stand firm that it's not an option. Hang the PCB in the area where you are providing the service or producing the product. Assign someone to fill the board out hourly and capture as much data as possible.

If nothing is done with the data collected on the board, your team will stop collecting data. Use the data to understand what is causing the problems and determine solutions to fix them.

Process Control Board

HR	Plan	Actual	Variance	Issue	Corrective Action
1					
2					
3					
4					
5					
6					
7					
8					
9					
10					

Sensei Questions

Can you name any processes for which you are responsible (or a key stakeholder) and that you're not satisfied with the performance?

_____

_____

_____

_____

_____

_____

Are you currently getting the data you need to understand why some processes are not performing to their potential?

_____

_____

_____

_____

_____

_____

Leadership

Since I have been consulting, I've been asked if I ever wanted to get back to management. It surprises some people when my answer is yes.

Back in my management days, I followed one simple concept: be firm, fair, and consistent. You can't and won't be liked by everyone. If you are, there's a good chance that you're not managing properly, and you may not be very effective.

Firm

You must be firm on rules, policies, and procedures and must follow standard work. It's not an option. I know that confronting people is uncomfortable, but you'll lose the respect of your team if you don't.

I'm not saying that you have to "run your ship with an iron fist." I've seen that style and, from my observations, it doesn't make the leader any more effective. It has an adverse effect with the team members, because they don't respect their leader.

Be steady as a leader. Demonstrate that you are solid, sturdy, and secure with your directions and decisions. Ensure that you have a well-balanced approach and are able to make things happen.

Fair

You must be fair and unbiased when addressing issues with your team members. Set expectations for the team as whole and for each individual member. Communicate these expectations to your team members. After you have done so, provide them with the resources needed to meet those expectations.

In order to be fair, you must "speak with data." Without speaking with data, what you say feels more like an opinion. This is why having some of the tools discussed is important. Having PCBs in place to capture data and conducting kamishibai audits provides data and shows whether your team members are following standard work.

The most critical characteristic is to *not* ask your team to do something that you're not willing to do yourself. You must walk the talk.

Consistent

Stay constant with your behavior and decisions, and don't be seen as wishy-washy.

Demonstrate to your team members that you are dependable and that they can count on you. For your team members, there's nothing worse than believing that their leader doesn't have their back. If they feel you won't stand up for them, they won't stick their neck out for you. It's a two-way street.

You can't have favorites. Everyone must be treated equally. So if people aren't meeting expectations and you have given them the resources to meet those expectations; coach and mentor them. I'm not sure how many chances you give on the mentoring phase, but in baseball, you get three strikes and you're out! If you get to this point, consult your human resources representative.

Managing a new way

When you embark on your Lean journey, it will require a new way to manage. You can't lead from your office. You'll need to be inside the gemba more so that you can see what is actually going on, not what you believe or hear.

It will require more rounding or going to the gemba to observe how your processes are performing. It will require you to walk the talk and lead by example!

I can only guess why leaders are reluctant to visit the gemba, and I assume that it's because they're not used to it. All the interaction might make them uncomfortable, but this is exactly what we are looking for: all the interaction. It's not just about being seen in the gemba. Interact with the team members to ensure that they have what they need, and help them address and solve the issues that arise.

Respect for People

One of the key attributes a Lean leader must demonstrate is respect for people. This characteristic includes empowering people to make decisions and change.

This new way of managing isn't for all leaders. There are leaders who are fast thinkers, quick decision makers, and excellent "fire fighters." They are excellent at what they do, but there's a lot to be said about working with a team of people versus one manager's ideas.

Who better to help solve the problems of the operations than the people performing the operations? The people who are performing the task are usually the ones who have great ideas on how to improve the task. Just ask. You'll earn their respect, and this will help you earn their trust.

Sensei Tip

To become an effective leader, you need to earn your team members trust. You should *not* ask them to do things that you're not willing to do, and you must be firm, fair, and consistent. Once you've earned their trust, they'll be willing to follow your vision, because they know that you have their back.

Sensei Questions

Name the characteristics of a good leader.

_____

_____

_____

_____

_____

_____

What's the difference between a manager and a leader?

_____

_____

_____

_____

_____

What would you change immediately to become a more effective leader?

_____

_____

_____

_____

_____

Leadership Daily Standard Work

———

The leadership daily standard work is not a detailed, step-by-step written document on how to perform a task. It is checklist of things that leaders must do in the course of their day to be effective Lean leaders.

When I'm coaching leaders on how to manage in a new way, this is a key component that I encourage them to incorporate. I often describe it as their "grocery list" of things to do. This list for managing in a new way should include the things that I have mentioned: gemba walks, kamishibai audits, PCB evaluations, team huddles, tiered huddles, etc.

As a leader, you must carry your daily standard work with you at all times.

The daily standard work form has an area for the leaders to record what they have discovered in the Gemba (see figure 15).

Leadership Daily Standard Work - Ops Manager						
Week: ___					Key Process Improvement Activity & Frequency	- Incomplete ☑ Complete
Mon	Tue	Wed	Thu	Fri	**Daily**	Actions, Observations and Questions
					MDI Huddle 07:05	
					Touch base w/Supr/Lead Tech	
					Leadership Huddle	
					Kamishibai Audit AM	
					Sterile Processing PCB AM	
					Daily Check in	
					Pharmacy Safety Huddle	
					Kamishibai Audit PM	
					Sterile Processing PCB PM	
					MDI Board update	
					MDI Huddle 13:25	
					Touch base with Supervisor	
Mon	Tue	Wed	Thu	Fri	**Weekly**	Actions, Observations and Questions
					Pharmacy Tactical Meeting	
					*VSA Steering Prep	
					VSA Steering Committee	
					*NDC Project Update	
					1:1 Tier huddle Next Level	
					In patient Pharmacy Gemba	
					Out patient Pharmacy Gemba	

Value Stream Managers

———

For value stream managers, standard work accounts for approximately a quarter of their time (not including regularly scheduled off-the-floor meetings). This includes leading a brief, structured huddle as part of the daily accountability process, just like team leaders and supervisors. The value stream manager's standard work includes gemba walks with each supervisor for teaching and inspecting the "homework," just as the supervisors' standard work includes gemba walking their team leaders. The balance of the value stream manager's gemba operations work calls for verifying execution of supervisors' standard work tasks. In this way, the value stream manager maintains his or her link in the chain of support for the integrity of operations.[7]

———

7 David W. Mann, *Creating a Lean Culture* (Boca Raton, FL: CRC Press, 2005), 34.

Sensei Tip

A leader's standard work differs from process standard work in one important respect. Leader standard work documents should be working documents. Leaders should have their standard work with them virtually all the time on a clipboard, printed on a card, in a daily planner, or in a PDA. The leaders should note completion of the indicated tasks on the standard work form. When they are unable to complete a task in sequence, on time, or at all, they should note it and record why. This is equivalent, and as important, as noting reasons for misses on performance-tracking charts. The notes should indicate when misses occurred in their areas and what action they took.[8]

---

8 David W. Mann, *Creating a Lean Culture* (Boca Raton, FL: CRC Press, 2005), 34.

Sensei Questions

Do you currently track your daily things to do, and if so, how?

_____
_____
_____
_____
_____
_____

After reading about what is encompassed in MDI, what elements would you add to your daily list of things to do?

_____
_____
_____
_____
_____

Are the people on your team following up with the tasks that are important to you? If not, list the items you would like more action on.

_____
_____
_____
_____
_____
_____

Problem Solving

Now that you have learned the components of MDI, it's time to graduate from information sharing to daily problem solving.

I have given you several ways to identify problems such as the following:

- A metric trended in the wrong direction on the MDI board.
- A missed performance or output appeared on a PCB.
- A team member brought up the issue at the daily huddle.
- A team member filled out a Golden Ticket about an issue.
- A kamishibai audit failed because a team member did not follow standard work.

The intent of MDI is to solve problems that are small. Do not try to solve world hunger or all problems at once. Work on one problem at a time.

The MDI huddle is the perfect place to begin the brainstorming process. Who better to recommend solutions to the problem than the people who experience it on a daily basis?

Some of the solutions will be a no-brainer and become a "just do it," but some may need to be confirmed and proven before being implemented. This is where your team will need to design an experiment to see if the solution works or not.

It's time to begin the Toyota eight-step problem-solving method:

1. Clarify the problem.
    a. State the "punch in the gut" problem statement.
    b. Confirm your problem statement with Pareto Analysis.
    c. Define the scope of the problem (trigger-done).

2. Break down the problem.
    a. Speak with data.
    b. Use the PICK chart to understand the difficulty and impact.
    c. Understand the what, when, where, and who.
    d. Create a flow map of the process.
    e. Identify the point of cause.

3. Set the target.
    a. Set a target for the point of cause.
    b. Determine "how much."
    c. Determine "by when."

4. Do a root cause analysis.
    a. Initiate the brainstorming process to learn the root cause.
    b. Use the Cause and Effect Diagram (Fishbone).
    c. Initiate the "Five Whys" process.

5. Develop countermeasures.
    a. Initiate the brainstorming process for solutions.

    b. Reach for seven alternatives.

    c. Narrow the alternatives using data and criteria.

    d. Gain consensus.

    e. Develop a detailed action plan.

6. See countermeasures through.
    a. Design experiments to test the solutions.
    b. Stress the process to fully test the solutions.
    c. Work the action plan.
    d. Confirm consensus.

7. Monitor the results and processes.
    a. Ensure that the new standard is followed.
    b. Evaluate the results.
    c. Track the data, and ensure that metrics are meeting the target.

8. Standardize successful processes.
    a. Share the results.
    b. Formalize the successful standard work.
    c. Initiate the next problem to solve.

Sensei Tip

The intent of MDI is to solve small, manageable issues that are affecting daily operations. If the issue is larger than the team or huddle can take on, the problem needs to be escalated to the next level of leadership. The next level of leadership may have to determine if the problem is big enough to start an A3 problem-solving initiative.

Sensei Questions

How do you currently go about solving problems on a daily basis?

_____

_____

_____

_____

_____

_____

Do you currently get input from your team members on how to solve problems? If so, what approach do you use? If not, why not?

_____

_____

_____

_____

_____

_____

Final Thoughts

———

There's an old-age question: "What came first, the chicken or the egg?" A similar question exist in a Lean implementation: "What comes first, Lean transformation initiatives or MDI?"

For the longest time, I believed that the Lean transformation was part of starting and working on value stream Lean transformation initiatives. Implementing the elements of MDI came second.

Several years ago, when working with a client, we did the opposite. Before starting value stream transformation work, we implemented the components of MDI, started the daily huddles, and began daily problem solving. I now believe that MDI is part of any Lean infrastructure and must be in place in order for transformation initiatives to stick.

When implementing MDI, it is okay (and highly recommended) to start with a narrow focus. You need to graduate to the balanced scorecard approach, but at the beginning, you may want to just focus on safety, quality, or delivery.

Remember to keep the huddles short (five to ten minutes). If they drag on longer, you'll be cutting into your productivity. Do not allow the huddles to become a complaint session; it's about solving problems, not complaining about them. Long huddles and complaint sessions are both counterproductive!

When you initiate the huddles, they'll be more of an informational sharing session. This allows the team to get comfortable with the process and promotes collaboration.

Once your unit is forming as a team and discussing daily operational issues, you can graduate to daily problem solving. Using balanced scorecard tracking on the board, conducting kamishibai audits and/or using the Golden Ticket process, you will identify the areas that need the most attention and resolve the daily issues that are causing operational problems.

About the Author

Robert Goldsmith has twenty-five years of experience in implementing continuous improvement through deploying Lean Six Sigma methods. His industry experience includes healthcare, medical equipment, government, defense, maintenance repair, and overhaul (MRO), automotive, and commercial.

Robert's career started at Hillenbrand Industries' Hill-Rom division. In twenty-one years at Hill-Rom, his career spanned from the shop floor to the value stream manager of acute care.

His Lean journey began in the late 1980s under the tutelage of TBM consulting and the Shingijutsu Group. Robert participated in over fifty kaizen events, developed shop floor metrics and visual management, and instituted policy deployment for his value stream.

In 2001, he accepted the role as director of operations at Herman Miller's Georgia division to lead a Lean transformation. During his time at Herman Miller, he continued developing his Lean understanding while working with Toyota Supplier Support Center (TSSC), which assisted Herman Miller in its journey.

In 2003, he was asked to join Simpler consulting as a senior consultant. In his nine years at Simpler, he conducted over five hundred consulting engagements in the areas of rapid improvement events, value stream analysis, problem solving, and training classes in bronze, silver, green and black belt training.

Leaning on his years of experience and coaching from recognized industry leaders, he formed VOC Lean Solutions, Inc. in 2012.

For the past seven years, he successfully transitioned from traditional manufacturing transformation to primarily supporting the healthcare segment.

His versatility has been instrumental in the development, delivery, and promotion of a variety of Lean programs. These have helped organizations accelerate Lean learning with a large number of people in a relatively short period of time.

His introduction to Managing for Daily Improvement (MDI) came during his tenure at the Hill-Rom Company. The MDI process followed the Toyota Production System methodology under the tutelage of TBM and Shingijutzu.

Made in the USA
Lexington, KY
19 April 2016